"The art of the subject stop"

Chad Bruckner

&

Nicholas Ruggiero

DEDICATION

"This book is dedicated to the man who showed me how to be a great Police Officer and Detective - my partner and big brother, Nick Oropeza."

- Chad

"The art"

Nicholas Ruggiero

The art of the subject stop is more than knowing when to stop a suspicious person(s) or knowing what case law allows you to facilitate the stop.

Above all else in this book is you and your fellow officers/deputy's physical safety. NEVER deviate from your training to protect your life or the life of the public. It's better to have the fruits of a poisonous tree thrown out in court than being carried by six of your closest friends or family.

That being said, a subject stop is truly an art and a dying art at that. Over the past few years, law enforcement agencies have encouraged officers to do less proactive

policing like subject stops because the risk of

a use of force is higher than ever.

In some aspects they are right. The chances

of having a use of force are greater because

the type of clientele you stopping has zero

regards for the law. In some cases, these are

multiple offenders with warrants already from

a very broken judicial system. That's neither

here nor there, your job is to catch the bad

guys and protect the public within the legal

confines of case law and articulation.

Articulation is a word you'll hear a million

times in the police academy and during your

field training. It's the only thing that will exonerate you if things go south or help you during prosecuting a criminal case. Many officers go to court and miss an incredible opportunity to sharpen their articulation skills without even testifying. Although the court can be cumbersome and to some a waste of time, it's a great opportunity to listen to prosecutors, judges, and defense attorneys articulate the law. This is like "Articulation for dummies".

In the case of Kyle Rittenhouse, one of the most profound parts of the trail was when he took the stand. Not because of his recount of the events of that night in May, but because as an 18-year-old kid he was exquisite in his articulation of self-defense. His understanding of what elements of self-defense was something that most 20-year law enforcement officers can't do. Yes, he was couched by his attorneys which is exactly my point. If an 18-year-old kid can learn the art of articulation then so can you. We can teach you all the techniques and tricks of the trade but ultimately you need to put the work into mastering your craft.

That being said, learning supreme court case law is one of if not the most important part of subject stops. You need to know cases that allow you to detain, search, and/or arrest based on decisions made by the courts.

Some of these cases will be outlined in this

book. You MUST read, understand, and keep

up with case law changes.

Case Law

*_Terry vs. Ohio._ Better known in our field as "Terry Stop". The concept of a Terry stop originated in the 1968 Supreme Court case _Terry v. Ohio_, in which a police officer detained three Cleveland men on the street behaving suspiciously as if they were preparing for armed robbery. The police conducted a pat-down search and discovered a revolver, and subsequently, two of the men were convicted of carrying a concealed weapon.[9] The men appealed their case to the Supreme Court, arguing that the revolver was found during an illegal search under the [1]Fourth Amendment. This brief detention and search were deemed

---

[1]*https://en.wikipedia.org/wiki/Terry_stop

admissible by the court, judging that the officer had reasonable suspicion which could be articulated (not just a hunch) that the person detained may be armed and dangerous. This was not mere "suspicion" but "reasonable suspicion" which could be articulated at a later date.[10]

This decision was made during a period of great social unrest in America in the 1960s, with rising crime, opposition to U.S. involvement in the Vietnam War and the civil rights movement, and race riots. It was thought that law enforcement needed to be provided with tools to deal with the unrest and new issues of urban crime. Some criticized the decision for watering down the prohibition against unreasonable searches and seizures; others praised it for balancing safety and individual rights.[10]:94

This case is our bread and butter, but very few really know what it means or allows us to do. So let's break it down. You're driving down Main Street around 0300hrs in an area where a series of commercial burglaries have occurred lately. No one is out except this lone person in a large jacket. Upon seeing you this person changes the direction of travel and walks the other way. Would this

constitute a reason to stop the person? If you

answered "No" please, please, please don't be

pushing a patrol car…. If you answered "Yes",

why? What gives you the right to stop this person?

Types of police-civilian encounters	
Consensual encounter	Requires neither probable cause nor reasonable suspicion
Terry stop (investigative detention)	Requires <u>reasonable suspicion</u>
Arrest	Requires <u>probable cause</u>

The answer to this scenario is actually a trick

question. First, yes you have every right to stop

this subject. Your reason falls into Terry vs. Ohio

because you have **Reasonable suspicion** that

crime may be about to occur based on previous

burglaries and the subject making suspicious

movements to avoid your attention. The other thing

about subject stops is the fact that you always

have the right to have a consensual encounter with

any person. This requires neither probable cause

nor reasonable suspicion and ends when the

person you're stopping breaks from the encounter.

This means if you have neither probable cause nor

reasonable suspicion and the person want to

leave, YOU MUST let them walk away. Get them

another day and don't end up on TikTok violating

someone's rights. Now that being said, if you have

reasonable suspicion or probable cause that

person is not free to go. Where most officers/

deputies go wrong is not knowing the difference

between detainment and an arrest. Also not

communicating to the person that they are not free

to go. Detainments don't always lead to an arrest

but knowing what legal right you have to hold

someone is key. A detainment must be a

"Reasonable amount of time". What's reasonable?

At some point, you need to shit or get off the pot

basically. If you're detaining someone for suspicion

of shoplifting, reviewing CCTV, and securing the

place of businesses willingness to prosecute takes

time and it's "reasonable" for it to take an extended

period of time. If you're detaining someone on

suspicion of burglary and none of the businesses

show signs of tampering and a "pat down"

produces negative results, it's time to let the bird

fly. Extending stops with no reasonable expectation

of criminal evidence is not only illegal but is a trick

bag for civil litigation. Civil attorneys have a field

day with law enforcement officers not knowing

what "reasonable suspicion" is and then keeping

people detained for an excessive amount of time.

I've worked with a lot of officers that have the

mentality that "they are free to go when I say they

can". Well, yes if you have a legitimate legal right

to hold them. If you don't and you're trying to fit a

round peg through a square hole to stick a charge,

then you're going to get jammed up. Stick to the

perimeters of Terry vs. Ohio. This case law gives

us an incredible amount of investigative power.

This includes a "Pat-down" on your subject. A pat-

down is exactly what it sounds like, patting your

subject down as the officers did in Terry. This

doesn't give you the right to dig in pockets like

you're in Alaska searching for gold. You can't

manipulate the pockets until something comes out

magically. Remember, you always have the ability

to ask for consent with the understanding that the

consent must be made freely and without threat or

intimidation. This is a concept that is heavily

litigated in court by defense attorneys. In some

arguments, any consent that was given while being

detained by the police is considered void or given

under direst. I've seen gun cases get tossed out

over this argument. Based on where you practice

law enforcement this may be an issue. In New York

City this because a major issue in 2019/2020

known as "Stop and frisk". NYPD officers were

getting a lot of illegal guns and drugs off the street

but were heavily criticized for the techniques used

to achieve the end results. The officers in almost all

of the cases had a legal right to detain and conduct

a pat-down on the subjects. In some cases, this

produced fruits of a possible crime or the possibility

of a crime occurring. The problem like most police

departments was the lack of articulation by the

Public Information Office on the law and right to

conduct searches. Educating the public on what

Terry vs. Ohio is could have alleviated some of the

bad press blowbacks. At least we would like it too.

<u>**United States v. Watson**</u>, 423 U.S. 411 (1976).

206 Henry v. United States, 361 U.S. 98 (1959); Johnson v. United States, 333 U.S. 10, 16–17 (1948); Sibron v. New York, 392 U.S. 40, 62–63 (1968).

207 "The police may not arrest upon mere suspicion but only on 'probable cause.'" Mallory v. United States, 354 U.S. 449, 454 (1957).

208 392 U.S. 1 (1968).

209 392 U.S. at 16. *See* id. at 16–20.

210 392 U.S. at 20, 21, 22.

211 392 U.S. at 23–27, 29. *See also* Sibron v. New York, 392 U.S. 40 (1968) (after policeman observed defendant speak with several known narcotics addicts, he approached him and placed[2]

---

his hand in defendant's pocket, thus discovering narcotics; this was impermissible, because he lacked a reasonable basis for the frisk and in any event his search exceeded the permissible scope of a weapons frisk); Adams v. Williams, 407 U.S. 143 (1972) (stop and frisk based on informer's in-person tip that defendant was sitting in an identified parked car, visible to informer and officer, in a high crime area at 2 a.m., with narcotics and a gun at his waist); Pennsylvania v. Mimms, 434 U.S. 106 (1977) (after validly stopping car, officer required defendant to get out of car, observed bulge under his jacket, and frisked him and seized weapon; while officer did not suspect driver of crime or have an articulable basis for safety fears, safety considerations justified his requiring driver to leave car);

Maryland v. Wilson, 519 U.S. 408, 413 (1997)

(after validly stopping car, officer may order

passengers as well as driver out of car; "the same

weighty interest in officer safety is present

regardless of whether the occupant of the

stopped car is a driver or passenger"); Arizona v.

Johnson, 129 S. Ct. 781, 786 (2009) (after validly

stopping car, officer may frisk (patdown for

weapons) both the driver and any passengers

whom he reasonably concludes "might be armed

and presently dangerous").

<u>**United States v. Cortez**</u>, 449 U.S. 411 (1981), a

unanimous Court attempted to capture the "elusive

concept" of the basis for permitting a stop. Officers

must have "articulable reasons" or "founded

suspicions," derived from the totality of the

circumstances. "Based upon that whole picture the

detaining officer must have a particularized and

objective basis for suspecting the particular person

stopped of criminal activity." Id. at 417–18. The

inquiry is thus quite fact-specific. In the anonymous

tip context, the same basic approach requiring

some corroboration applies regardless of whether

the standard is probable cause or reasonable

suspicion; the difference is that less information, or

less reliable information, can satisfy the lower

standard. Alabama v. White, 496 U.S. 325 (1990).

Brown v. Texas, 443 U.S. 47 (1979)
(individual's presence in high crime area gave
officer no articulable basis to suspect him of
crime); **Delaware v. Prouse**, 440 U.S. 648
(1979) (reasonable suspicion of a license or
registration violation is necessary to authorize
automobile stop; random stops
impermissible); United States v. Brignoni-
Ponce, 422 U.S. 873 (1975) (officers could not
justify random automobile stop solely on basis
of Mexican appearance of occupants); Reid v.
Georgia, 448 U.S. 438 (1980) (no reasonable
suspicion for airport stop based on
appearance that suspect and another

passenger were trying to conceal the fact that

they were traveling together). *But cf.* United

States v. Martinez-Fuerte, 428 U.S. 543

(1976) (halting vehicles at fixed checkpoints to

question occupants as to citizenship and

immigration status permissible, even if officers

should act on basis of the appearance of

occupants).

Brendlin v. California -

551 U.S. 249, 127 S. Ct. 2400 (2007)

RULE:

A person is seized by the police and thus

entitled to challenge the government's action

under the Fourth Amendment when the officer,

by means of physical force or show of

authority, terminates or restrains his freedom

of movement through means intentionally

applied. Thus, an unintended person may be

the object of the detention, so long as the

detention is willful and not merely the

consequence of an unknowing act. A police

officer may make a seizure by a show of

authority and without the use of physical force,

but there is no seizure without actual submission; otherwise, there is at most an attempted seizure, so far as the Fourth Amendment is concerned.

FACTS:

After officers stopped a car to check its registration without reason to believe it was being operated unlawfully, one of them recognized defendant, a passenger in the car. Upon verifying that defendant was a parole violator, the officers formally arrested him and searched him, the driver, and the car, finding, among other things, methamphetamine paraphernalia. Defendant was charged with various methamphetamine offenses, and he moved to suppress the evidence obtained in the searches of his person and the car as fruits of an unconstitutional seizure. The State conceded that the police had no adequate justification to pull the car over. The Supreme Court of California held suppression was unwarranted as the defendant was a passenger. Certiorari was granted to decide whether a traffic stop subjected a passenger, as well as the driver, to Fourth Amendment seizure.

TENNESSEE V. NICHOLSON[3]

Defendant, James D. Nicholson, following his guilty plea to possession of cocaine for resale: "whether the evidence seized from the defendant, in this case, should have been suppressed because it was seized pursuant to the warrantless arrest of the defendant for which the police had no probable cause in violation of the 4th Amendment to the United States Constitution and Article One, Section Seven of the Tennessee Constitution as well as the Tennessee Supreme Court's decision in State of Tennessee v. Perry Thomas

---

[3] https://www.tncourts.gov/courts/supreme-court/
opinions/2006/04/17/state-tennessee-v-james-d-
nicholson

Randolph, 74 S.W.3d 330 (Tenn. 2002)." After

being instructed to "hold up" by a detective,

Defendant turned and ran. A majority of the

Court of Criminal Appeals concluded that

Defendant was seized when he was thereafter

pursued and apprehended by officers. The

intermediate court concluded that, because

the detectives lacked reasonable suspicion or

probable cause to effectuate such a seizure,

the evidence flowing therefrom must be

suppressed. After careful review of the record

and applicable authority, we concur with the

judgment rendered by the Court of Criminal

Appeals. Accordingly, we affirm the judgment

of the Court of Criminal Appeals, reverse and

vacate Defendant's conviction and dismiss the

charges. We also emphasize the importance

of creating an adequate record for review in

cases such as this one.

ILLINOIS *v.* WARDLOW

No. 98—1036. Argued November 2, 1999—

Decided January 12, 2000

Respondent Wardlow fled upon seeing a

caravan of police vehicles converge on an

area of Chicago known for heavy narcotics

trafficking. When Officers Nolan and Harvey

caught up with him on the street, Nolan

stopped him and conducted a protective pat-

down search for weapons because in his

experience there were usually weapons in the

vicinity of narcotics transactions. Discovering

a handgun, the officers arrested Wardlow. The

Illinois trial court denied his motion to

suppress, finding the gun was recovered during a lawful stop and frisk. He was convicted of unlawful use of a weapon by a felon. In reversing, the State Appellate Court found that Nolan did not have reasonable suspicion to make the stop under *Terry* v. *Ohio,* 392 U.S. 1. The State Supreme Court affirmed, determining that sudden flight in a high crime area does not create a reasonable suspicion justifying a *Terry* stop because flight may simply be an exercise of the right to "go on one's way," see *Florida* v. *Royer,* 460 U.S. 491.

Held: The officers' actions did not violate the Fourth Amendment. This case, involving a brief encounter between a citizen and a police

officer on a public street, is governed by *Terry,*

under which an officer who has a reasonable,

articulable suspicion that criminal activity is

afoot may conduct a brief, investigatory stop.

While "reasonable suspicion" is a less

demanding standard than probable cause,

there must be at least a minimal level of

objective justification for the stop. An

individual's presence in a "high crime area,"

standing alone, is not enough to support a

reasonable, particularized suspicion of

criminal activity, but a location's

characteristics are relevant in determining

whether the circumstances are sufficiently

suspicious to warrant further investigation,

Adams v. *Williams,* 407 U.S. 143, 144, 147—

148. In this case, moreover, it was also

Wardlow's unprovoked flight that aroused the

officers' suspicion. Nervous, evasive behavior

is another pertinent factor in determining

reasonable suspicion, *e.g., United States* v.

Brignoni-Ponce, 422 U.S. 873, 885, and

headlong flight is the consummate act of

evasion. In reviewing the propriety of an

officer's conduct, courts do not have available

empirical studies dealing with inferences from

suspicious behavior, and this Court cannot

reasonably demand scientific certainty when

none exists. Thus, the reasonable suspicion

determination must be based on commonsense judgments and inferences about human behavior. See *United States* v. *Cortez,* 449 U.S. 411, 418. Officer Nolan was justified in suspecting that Wardlow was involved in criminal activity, and, therefore, in investigating further. Such a holding is consistent with the decision in *Florida* v. *Royer, supra,* at 498, that an individual, when approached, has a right to ignore the police and go about his business. Unprovoked flight is the exact opposite of "going about one's business." While flight is not necessarily indicative of ongoing criminal activity, *Terry* recognized that officers can detain individuals to resolve ambiguities in their conduct, 392 U.S., at 30, and thus accepts the risk that officers may stop innocent people. If they do not learn facts rising to the level of probable cause, an individual must be allowed to go on his way. But in this case the officers found that Wardlow possessed a handgun and arrested him for violating a state law. The propriety of that arrest is not before the Court. Pp. 3—6.

183 Ill. 2d 306, 701 N. E. 2d 484, reversed and remanded.

Rehnquist, C. J., delivered the opinion of the Court, in which O'Connor, Scalia, Kennedy, and Thomas, JJ., joined. Stevens, J., filed an an opinion concurring in part and dissenting in part, in which Souter, Ginsburg, and Breyer, JJ., joined.

"Hands kill"

If you haven't been told the term, "Hands kill"
then hear it now. They do!

Watching and controlling the hands of
violators, suspects, and persons detained is
the pinnacle of officer safety. If you become
complacent and/or don't watch the hands of
every person you interact with, start!

Every good subject stop requires you to
command your encounter. Even if you didn't
initiate the subject stop, you need to ensure
that you command the stop. Establish the
control from the start of the start. "Hey Sir/
Miss, please keep your hands out of your

pockets so I can see them while we speak, unless I pat you down". This establishes your expectations on that person and/or can give you consent to search with having probable cause. How? It's human nature to do what you are asked not to do and to want approval. When you tell the person being stopped, "Don't do X, unless I pat you down" physiologically they want your approval in most cases (not all the time), this must be used to your advantage to gain consent to search. Any fruits of this search that are made freely and with consent are admissible in court.

Where officers make the mistake is beating around the bush. Many officers would rather say, "Take your hands out of your pocket" a million times than say once, "Unless I can search you". This only works when it's done correctly and following search and seizure laws.

Like I've said before, your script must be flawless and consistent when you do subject stops. You need to practice asking for consent over and over so it's second nature. Ask for consent even when you don't want to search. I spoke about this is "The traffic stop" extensively. Asking for consent from the mom in a soccer van to the gang banger riding dirty.

Yes, you will be rejected a lot, or you will be

challenged on your reasoning. You must be

able to articulate your reasoning on the street

and on the witness stand. Know the case law

that allows you to control the movements of

violators, suspects, and/or detainees.

Hands can't shoot you or assault you if they

are occupied or under control. Detainment is

an excellent way to limit someone's

movements with their hands. Don't be afraid

to handcuff someone and say, "You're not

under arrest, right now I'm just detaining you".

Make sure your reason for detainment is valid

and covered under good faith/department

policy. Understand that if you detain someone

and you don't have a legitimate reason and it

goes sideways, your going to take the internal

investigation ride.

Chapter 1: Introduction

Chad Bruckner

In 1829, Sir Robert Peel formed the first metropolitan police department in London, England. Since that time, policing in democratic societies has been as controversial as it has been rewarding. Police officers patrolling our communities have been tasked with difficult assignments to protect our communities while also forging close bonds with its' citizens. The two objectives are seemingly in conflict with one another.

Our citizens want to feel safe and often do not understand the methods law enforcement officers need to utilize to keep them safe. Ask any current or former police officer the best way to reduce and prevent crime and they will tell you it's 'boots on the ground' stopping vehicles and people that appear and act suspiciously. Thus, in lies the conflict. Not every pedestrian suspicious stop leads to an arrest. Not every vehicle stopped is occupied by a felon. In fact, most police/citizen encounters result in no formal action taken. Yet, patrol officers are tasked with sniffing out suspicious activity and keeping vigil for criminality in our communities. If there is a skill a seasoned patrol officer possesses, it's the ability to quickly identify suspicious activity. They know when something is amiss. After all, they are professionals and that is their job. Some people refer to police officers as protectors or warriors; however, I prefer "guardians." They are in our communities 24 hours a day, often the only line between civil obedience and criminal behavior. Yet, most of their duties involve "community policing" activities aimed at forging strong relationships and trust between citizens and law enforcement agencies.

We all have memories of watching the news when there were stories involving police brutality. We recall where we were and who we were with. Whether it was Rodney King in Los Angeles in 1991 or Michael Brown in Ferguson, Missouri in 2014, these events made headlines and reverberated within all police agencies. They dictate policy change, affected culture and morale, and certainly altered relationships and trust between our citizens and guardians. There has always been an ebb and flow of citizen satisfaction and appreciation toward law enforcement. Depending on your age, race, where you reside, or socioeconomic factors, you have a different opinion on the police. Yet undoubtedly – when a serious crime occurs in our communities the police must explain what they are doing to investigate, mitigate and prevent crime. It can be a conundrum for law enforcement to effectively prevent crime and respect citizens' rights and expectations simultaneously. The challenges were further heightened in 2020 following the death of George Floyd at the hands of a police officer in Minneapolis, MN. There was rioting, targeting of police officers' homes, and the distrust of law enforcement was never higher in the past 50 years.

Chapter 2: How to be a Quality Police Officer

21st Century Policing

I was a patrol supervisor in 2020 serving in an affluent county just outside of Philadelphia, PA. I experienced the protests and riots. Most were peaceful but some were not. People were angry, rightfully so – but what I saw was a change in how police officers were doing their job. I was a cop for 13 years and was viewed as a proactive officer. I made hundreds of arrests for serious crimes that negatively affected the community. However, I never had one complaint about using inappropriate/illegal force or engaging in aggressive activity to the degree that it offended citizens. As a matter of fact, I received compliments and acknowledgments from residents and business owners of how

kind, down-to-earth and helpful I conducted
myself.

There are three fundamental reasons
why this happened. First, I understood the
law, procedural justice, and my department's
policy inside and out. Second, I practiced the
Golden Rule in every citizen encounter. I
treated citizens with courtesy and respect like
I would treat my grandmother or a neighbor.
Third, I live by a strict set of core values that
guide me to protect and serve with integrity
and fidelity. I highlight this for one main
reason, if you are embarking on a law
enforcement career and you pledge to give
maximum effort to your community, then

proactive policing is necessary for our

communities to be safe. If you conduct

yourself the right way, there is no reason to

fear repercussions from wrongdoing. Follow

this book and let it guide you, but you must

learn to walk before you can run. We will

outline the rules a proactive police officer must

follow and the techniques that will help you

become a successful proactive patrol officer

while also building strong relationships with

your communities. First, let's cover the **10**

Core Ethos that is <u>**non-negotiable**</u>.

1) Commit yourself to living and serving

virtuously.

2) Fully comprehend your state laws and agency policies and procedures.

3) Be humble, kill your ego (ego is the death of duty).

4) Become a "professional" by practicing for thousands of hours on every task you want to be great at (and hundreds of hours on everything else).

5) Never forget that your role in society is as a citizen first, Police Officer second (you are them and they are you).

6) Ask a lot of questions of your Senior Officers (remember humility – it's OK to not know something, but it's never OK not to learn something).

7) Find the best Officer in your agency and become his/her best friend (don't worry about copycatting, she/he learned from someone else too).

8) Don't be afraid to try new things, that's how we grow and evolve (stagnation and complacency are career killers).

9) You can't get "training and experience" without going to training and gaining experience, so try everything.

10) Manage your expectations and keep them reasonable (the world doesn't meet anyone halfway - if you want something you have to go after it).

If you follow these 10 Core Ethos, you will be solid in proactive policing. Greatness will come by being consistent and demonstrating a growth mindset. Expertise will occur when you begin to accomplish things that no one at your agency has done before. Keep growing, don't stop!

Skills/Traits Necessary for Proactive Policing

1) Communication

2) Patient

3) Curious

4) Calm

5) Confidence

6) Desire

7) Humility

8) Relationship builder

9) Consistency

10) Likability

Dr. Tommy Karam is a Louisiana State University Professor and media coach to professional athletes such as Drew Brees and Shaquille O'Neal. Dr. Tommy Karam has long advocated that likability more than any other character trait is what enables people to like us and comply with us. Further, Dr. Karam states that 2/3 of negotiations come down to likability. In short, if people like us then we are more likely to gain their compliance and cooperation. Do you know any other professions where people are interacting daily with other people attempting to get them to do what they're requested? Yes, Police Officers!

<u>Chapter 3: Compliance</u>

The name of the game in Law Enforcement is compliance. Every day Police Officers are requesting or demanding compliance from the citizens we serve. One of the most common complaints citizens have against Police Officers is the tone and attitude of the officers. When you realize that you'll get more with honey than vinegar, you're halfway on the road to compliance.

How do we get compliance? To answer that we need to reflect on our authority as Police Officers. Just because we're legally authorized to demand something from a citizen doesn't mean we get to do so at any cost. Remember, it's all about the endgame.

Let's dive deeper into the 2 basic strategies

for authority - control and influence.

Power of _control_: Using coercion, threats,

force, or the perception of power to gain

compliance or obedience; the power to do

something to someone.

Power of _influence_: Using one's honor and

principles to earn people's respect and make

a positive difference in their lives; the power to

work effectively with others to get a better

result.

I'm sure you're reaching that and asking

yourself what control and influence have to do

with compliance. Getting compliance from

other human beings is not as easy as you
think. God created us with free will and the
ability to make willfully make our own choices.
Whether it's in leadership, parenting, or
coaching, gaining compliance from people is
nothing more than "buying in." How do we get
people to buy-in? Well, it's much easier if we
influence them rather than *control* them. It is
no different from citizens on the street. Too
many Police Officers use control tactics to
gain compliance. That will work on violent
prisoners, but it won't work on citizens on the
street.

We get people to do what WE want them to
do through influence. We treat people

respectfully, aim to be a positive light, and bring people into our circle as collaborators, not dissenters. Let's talk about pedestrian and subject stops!

Chapter 4: The Law and Mechanics of Pedestrian/Subject Stops

The art of the subject stop is more than knowing when to stop a suspicious person(s) or knowing what case law allows you to facilitate the stop. Above all else in this book is you and your fellow officers/deputies' physical safety. NEVER deviate from your training to protect your life or the life of the public. It's better to have the fruits of a poisonous tree thrown out in court than to be carried by six of your closest friends or family.

That being said, a subject stop is truly an art and a dying art at that. Over the past few years law enforcement agencies have

encouraged officers to do less proactive

policing like subject stops because the risk of

a use of force is higher than ever.

In some aspects they are right. The

chances of having a use of force

complaint are greater because some of

the citizens you will be stopping have

minimal regard for the law. In some

cases, these are multiple offenders with

warrants already from a broken judicial

system. The criminal justice will be

discussed in another book. Your job is to

prevent crime by catching the bad guys

and protecting the public within the legal

confines of case law and articulation.

Articulation is a word you'll hear a million

times in the police academy and during

your

field training. It's the only thing that will

exonerate you if things go south or help

you during prosecuting a criminal case.

Many officers go to court and miss an

incredible opportunity to sharpen their

articulation skills without even testifying.

Although the court can be cumbersome

and to some a waste of time, it's a great

opportunity to listen to prosecutors,

judges, and defense attorneys articulate

the law. This is like "Articulation for

dummies".

In the case of Kyle Rittenhouse, one of

the most profound parts of the trail was

when he took the stand. Not because of

his recount of the events of that night in

May, but because

at an 18-year-old kid, he was exquisite in

his articulation of self-defense. His

understanding of what elements of self-

defense was something that most 20-year

law enforcement officers can't do. Yes,

he was couched by his attorneys which is

exactly my point. If an 18-year-old kid can learn the art of articulation then so can you. We can teach you all the techniques and tricks of the trade but ultimately you need to put the work into mastering your craft.

That being said, learning supreme court case law is one of if not the most important part of subject stops. You need to know cases that allow you to detain, search, and/or arrest based on decisions made by the courts.

Cases like *Terry vs. Ohio.* Better known in our field as "Terry Stop". The concept of a Terry stop originated in the 1968 Supreme Court case *Terry v. Ohio*, in which a police officer detained three Cleveland men on the street behaving suspiciously as if they were preparing for armed robbery. The police conducted a pat-down search and discovered a revolver, and subsequently, two of the men were convicted of carrying a concealed weapon.[9] The men appealed their case to the Supreme Court, arguing that the revolver was found during an illegal search under the

[1]Fourth Amendment. This brief detention and search were deemed admissible by the court, judging that the officer had reasonable suspicion which could be articulated (not just a hunch) that the person detained may be armed and dangerous. This was not mere "suspicion" but "reasonable suspicion" which could be articulated at a later date.

[10]

This decision was made during a period of great social unrest in America in the 1960s, with rising crime, opposition to U.S. involvement in the Vietnam War and the civil rights movement, and race riots. It was thought that law enforcement needed to be provided with tools to deal with the unrest and

[1]*https://en.wikipedia.org/wiki/Terry_stop

new issues of urban crime. Some criticized the decision for watering down the prohibition against unreasonable searches and seizures; others praised it for balancing safety and individual rights.[10]:94

This case is our bread and butter, but very few really know what it means or allows us to do. So let's break it down. You're driving down Main Street around 0300hrs in an area where a series of commercial burglaries have occurred lately. No one is out except for this lone person in a large jacket.

Upon seeing you this person changes the direction of travel and walks the other way. Would this constitute a reason to stop the person? If you answered "No" please, please, please don't be pushing a patrol car…. If you answered "Yes", why? What gives you the right to stop this person?

Types of police-civilian encounters	
Consensual encounter	Requires neither probablecause nor reasonable suspicion
Terry stop (investigative detention)	Requires reasonable suspicion
Arrest	Requires probable cause

The answer to this scenario is actually a trick

question. First, yes you have every right to stop this subject. Your reason falls into Terry vs. Ohio because you have **Reasonable suspicion** that a crime may be about to occur based on previous burglaries and the subject making suspicious movements to avoid your attention. The other thing about subject stops is the fact that you always have the right to have a consensual encounter with any person. This requires neither probable cause nor reasonable suspicion and ends when the person you're stopping breaks from the encounter. This means if you have neither probable cause nor reasonable suspicion and the person want to leave, YOU MUST let them walk away. Get them another day and don't end up on TikTok violating someone's rights. Now that being said, if you have reasonable suspicion or probable cause that person is not free to go. Where most officers/ deputies go wrong is not knowing the difference between detainment and an arrest. Also, not communicating to the person that they are not free to go. Detainments don't always lead to an arrest but knowing what legal right you have to hold someone is key. A detainment must be a "Reasonable amount of time". What's reasonable?

At some point, you need to shit or get off the pot basically. If you're detaining someone for suspicion of shoplifting, reviewing CCTV, and securing the place of businesses willingness to prosecute takes time and it's "reasonable" for it to take an extended period of time. If you're detaining someone on suspicion of burglary and none of the businesses show signs of tampering and a "pat down" produces negative results, it's time to let the bird fly. Extending stops with no reasonable expectation of criminal evidence is not only illegal but is a trick bag for civil litigation. Civil attorneys have a field day with law enforcement officers not knowing what "reasonable suspicion" is and then keeping people detained for an excessive amount of time.

I've worked with a lot of officers that have the mentality that "they are free to go when I say they can". Well, yes if you have a legitimate legal right to hold them. If you don't and you're trying to fit a round peg through a square hole to stick a charge, then you're going to get jammed up. Stick to the perimeters of Terry vs. Ohio. This case law gives us an incredible amount of investigative power. This includes a "Pat-down" on your subject. A pat-down is exactly what it sounds like, patting your subject down as the officers did in Terry. This doesn't give you the right to dig in pockets like you're in Alaska searching for gold. You can't manipulate the pockets until something comes out magically. Remember, you always have the ability to ask for consent with the understanding that the consent must be made freely and without threat or intimidation. This is a concept that is heavily litigated in court by defense attorneys.

In some arguments, any consent that was given while being detained by the police is considered void or given under direst. I've seen gun cases get tossed out over this argument. Based on where you practice law enforcement this may be an issue. In New York City this because a major issue in 2019/2020 known as "Stop and frisk". NYPD officers were getting a lot of illegal guns and drugs off the street but were heavily criticized for the techniques used to achieve the end results. The officers in almost all of the cases had a legal right to detain and conduct a pat-down on the subjects. In some cases, this produced fruits of a possible crime or the possibility of a crime occurring. The problem like most police departments was the lack of articulation by the Public Information Office on the law and right to conduct searches. Educating the public on

what Terry vs. Ohio is could have alleviated

some of the bad press blowbacks. At least we

would like it too.

Chapter 5: Techniques & Tactics

Whether you observed suspicious activity or believe criminality is afoot, there are factors you should consider before making the stop. Like any other tactic, the more you practice the better you'll become. The skills necessary to stop citizens and engage in productive conversations that result in compliance are perishable, meaning that you will lose your edge if not consistent. Before you make your stop, it is always good to have a plan in your head. Rushing into the stop is problematic and decreases your chance of a successful outcome.

Remember, once you have reasonable suspicion to make a stop it is up to you to decide where, when, and how to make the subject stop. If the environment is not conducive to the stop, wait until the subject is further away from the area. If the pedestrian gets into a vehicle, then that will alter your plan. It's best to dry run different scenarios in your head while on patrol so in the event the situation presents itself, you already have thought about how you will conduct the stop. We will run through some common examples of suspicious activity and outline how we recommend executing the stop.

Chapter 6 – Drug Activity

It's 3 AM and you are on patrol. You're driving past a location well known for drug activity and other illegal activities, such as a gas station and bar, when you see a person on foot meet with a car that just pulled up. The subject reached into the vehicle and appeared to exchange items with the driver. Moments later, the vehicle departs and the subject walks away in the opposite direction. What suspicious behaviors did you observe? First, you have prior knowledge that drug activity/ arrests have occurred at this location in the past. Second, your knowledge of drug activity taught you that drug deals are generally brief, and the parties tend to

leave abruptly and away from each other.

Third, you know from your training,

experience and education that reaching

into a car and exchanging something and

perhaps putting that item into your pocket

could be indicative of a drug deal. Any of

these issues by themselves is probably

not enough reasonable suspicious to

make a stop, but when you stack them up

and execute a proper decision-making

process, you now have reasonable

suspicion to make a stop. Further,

perhaps you ran the vehicle registration

as it pulled away and you learned that the

registered owner was arrested 6 months

earlier for Possession With the Intent to

Deliver Controlled Substances.

When deciding on whom to stop, the

vehicle or the pedestrian, it's always

recommended to think several steps

down the line. Making emotional or rash

decisions rarely work out and that is

certainly true in law enforcement. Some

may suggest stopping the vehicle

because that is the suspected drug

dealer. However, what if you stop the

vehicle and find nothing? Now you lost

the initiative, and the driver knows you are

on to him. We recommend stopping the

pedestrian. First, he's on foot so time is

on your side. Second, it's safer than stopping a vehicle. Most importantly, the risk/reward is in your favor. If you find narcotics on the subject, you now have an opportunity to 'flip' the subject and cultivate a drug informant. Not only will you make an arrest and take dangerous substances off the street, but you will have an opportunity to work higher up the ladder and go after the source. Remember, the drug dealer may only be a middleman and he/she obtained the drugs from someone. The worst-case scenario is that you don't recover narcotics and the subject is not cooperative. There's always tomorrow.

Let's say you want to stop the vehicle. It's

critical to pick a location convenient for

YOU. It's also best to notify other Officers

of your intentions so they can start

moving toward your location to assist.

Last, the most important part is deciding

what and how you're going to

communicate with the driver. It would be

unwise to run-up to the vehicle and yell at

the driver "Where are the drugs?!"

Instead, treat it like every other vehicle

stop. Remember, the driver does not

know everything you know. He may

assume it's related to his encounter with

the subject at the gas station or he may

be concerned that his license is invalid.

The point is you dictate your demeanor,

tone, and tactics. Never compromise

strategy because you're ramped up to

seize narcotics. Be calm, poised, and

deliberate. There is nothing wrong with

advising the driver of an alternate

narrative that gives you access to the car

or gives you additional time to process

your decision. I used to deploy ruses or

pre-texts that were believable and

practical. That way I would not blow my

story but most importantly put the driver at

ease because he/she thinks you stopped

them for a different reason. For example, I

routinely deployed "the crackdown of child

pornography." I had a great story based on real statistics on how the internet has changed the ease of manufacturing, producing, and sharing child pornography. Child pornography media could be on USB flash drives or DVDs and easily concealable. Most notably, no one wants to be associated with child pornography so almost every human being will vehemently deny possessing child pornography. This ruse was effective in gaining the attention of the operator while also disarming their paranoia. "Bro, I don't have child pornography in my car!" the operator exclaims. Use the operator's passion and denials to your advantage and ask for consent to search the vehicle.

You will be surprised how many operators

give you consent. During the entire

encounter, you should be conversational

and collaborative. The more you engage

with the operator and cultivate the

relationship, the less suspicious they will

be of you and they will also be distracted

from your search because of your

engagement with them. Like everything

else in policing, the more humble, likable,

and engaging you are,

the easier everything is.

Chapter 7 – Property Crimes

It's 2 PM on a Saturday afternoon and you're on patrol. You drive past a recently foreclosed, locked business. As you turn down the rear alley to check the rear of the building, you see a subject looking in the rear windows. As you approach, the subject notices you and walks away briskly. What are you going to do? Do you have enough reasonable suspicion to stop the subject? Of course, you do! Here's where many Officers make a crucial mistake. They formed a judgment that crime is afoot, and the entire encounter suffers because of the Officer's judgment. Remember to be CURIOUS.

You truly don't know what the subject is

up to, but you know the business is

closed and the subject is looking in the

rear windows of the business. Just by

those observations, you absolutely have

reasonable suspicion to stop the subject

and inquire about his/her actions. Use this

as an opportunity to build a relationship

with the subject. You don't have to be

adversarial and accusatory, not yet at

least. Ask questions, foster conversation,

be open-minded and demonstrate

patience. Just by being inquisitive, you're

creating a safe space for the subject, and

they will be less defensive. Further, it

gives you additional time to think on your feet and assess your options. Time is your friend. Perhaps the subject makes statements that lead you to ask for consent to search their person. Their compliance will be significantly higher if you make them a part of the discussion.

<u>Chapter 8 – Mere Encounters</u>

The most challenging pedestrian stop to make is 'mere encounters.' A mere encounter is an interaction with a citizen in which a reasonable person feels free to leave. This could be a customer at the convenience store or someone taking a walk in a park. People doing everyday things and encounter Police Officers. We hope these interactions are positive but highly skilled Officers can use a mere encounter interaction as a technique for crime prevention in the form of proactive policing. Here's the trick – you don't want them to believe the encounter is anything other than chance. Easier said than done but it is certainly possible and if practiced consistently you can become a master.

For example, you're parked in a shopping

center parking lot on a Friday night

reading reports on your Mobile Data

Terminal (MDT). It's summer and your

windows are down. You hear the

commotion coming from a nearby

apartment complex parking lot and you

get out of your patrol vehicle to

investigate on foot. As you covertly stand

behind trees or bushes, you see a group

of twenty-somethings drinking beer in the

lot and one of the males is pulling on car

door handles checking for unlocked cars.

Whether you're a seasoned Officer or

rookie, you're aware that people check for

unlocked door handles with the intent of

stealing the contents within the vehicle.

As you look around the lot you notice 2

unoccupied cars with their dome lights on.

You assume that they were entered

illegally and you're now investigating

suspected theft. What do you do?

You could run into the lot and yell "Police!"

Everyone would scatter and your job just

got infinitely harder. You could sneak up

on them and catch them with open liquor

containers on private property. Or you

could use wit, grit, and a desire to work

smarter not harder (yes!). Whether you

get back into your car or approach the

group on foot is dependent upon staffing

levels, Municipality size, distance,

topography, and other issues to consider.

Develop an objective that you want to

complete. In this case, it's investigating

and solving the thefts from vehicles which

you believed occurred based on the

illuminated dome lights and subject

pulling on door handles. With that

objective in mind, you'll not only stay on

task easier, but it will help you focus on

the end goal. Let's say you approach on

foot to use the element of surprise. As you

approach, you confirmed the group is

drinking alcohol. Forget the open

containers, noise complaints, and

possible underage drinkers. You can

circle back on those later, if necessary,

but focusing on minor issues hinders your

chances of solving the bigger one.

Remember, they don't know what you

observed. Their first instinct is to protect

themselves from getting into trouble from

drinking in the lot. Let them! They don't

realize you're goal is to search the subject

you observed pulling on car door handles.

Remember likeability? Smile and make a

joke. Get them to laugh and create an

environment where you're not a form of

authority. Self-deprecation and humility go

a long way. The goal is for them to feel

comfortable while you conduct your

investigation. You've locked in on the subject you observed pulling on car door handles. You're asking for personal details about him/her in an effort to build a relationship. You could be telling corny jokes or cool police stories. All the while, you should be visually inspecting his wardrobe for any bulges. You're looking for signs of theft or guilty non-verbal behavior. Time is on your side be deliberate and patient. When your gut tells you that this subject indeed probably stole items from the cars, it is now time to ask him/her for consent to search their person. This is where being an effective communicator is a superpower. Your goal is to be assertive and confident while being equally friendly and trustworthy. The subject *knows* they entered the car and stole items, but he/she doesn't know that you *know* that. If you built a positive rapport properly, he/she doesn't want to upset you so they will do everything possible to be agreeable. Use that to your advantage. Be coy and draw attention to the fact that you noticed the dome lights are on. Ask the group if they know anything about it. Be direct with the suspect, who is now hopefully your 'friend,' and ask him/her directly if they know. Ask for their help. From my experience, he/she may even offer to help you find who did it. Maybe not. Once you feel you're ready, use your **influence** to gain their compliance. Ask the group if you could search them to rule them out as suspects. This accomplishes two things, first, it further strengthens your relationship with them because they think you're not considering them suspects. Second, you're making them part of the team! Nothing makes people comply better when they believe their honorary Police Officers. Most of the time, they will comply and consent to the search because you're kind, friendly, and likable. You're negotiating compliance and as Dr. Karam said 2/3 successful negotiations come down to likability. The most

important part of this particular negotiation

is that the subject is not aware you

suspect him. You've disarmed him and he

will be pleasantly agreeable to your

request. With your skills (and a little luck),

you'll recover stolen property and the

subject may even apologize to you

because he/she will feel they let you

down!